The Basics of Managing Money

Keep it Simple to Build Savings

Published by Jane N. Hughes Melbourne, Victoria

ISBN: 978-0-6488978-3-5

Edited by Anne Schmitt & Dr. Christopher Ringrose
Cover photo by Brian Hughes
Cover design by Jane N . Hughes & Brian Hughes
Interior design by Jane N . Hughes

Disclaimer:

The author of this book is neither a registered financial advisor, nor a stockbroker and any content provided in the book is for general information purposes only. Therefore, this information should not be treated as a substitute for advice on personal investments. Any decision made regarding all investments is solely the responsibility of the individual. The author shall not be reliable in respect of claims, damages or loss in connection to the information gained from this book. The names and characters used in this book are fictional.

website: janenhughes.com

The Basics of Managing Money

Keep it Simple to Build Savings

JANE N. HUGHES

Contents

Section Five

Section Six

Section Seven

Section Eight

Section Nine

Section Ten

Section One

Introduction

You work in a job where the pay is well regulated, but nevertheless you find that many of your colleagues live pay packet to pay packet. You often wonder why this is the case and why so many people are in such a position, but the cause becomes very apparent when you hear about the lifestyles they pursue. It is evident that unless they put their finances in order this problem will continue indefinitely.

Managing money is such a big issue that people seek to pay off a debt with one bank card while incurring debt on another. This begins a common and vicious circle of paying debts without clearing them. The following example is a summary of an interaction you might have had with a colleague. Let's call her Jill. Jill approached you while at work and this is her story.

Jill: Hi Jane, how are you doing?

Jane: Good, thank you Jill - and you?

Jill: Well, it seems like I am always busy working fulltime but managing my money is another story. Might I please share my problems with you?

Jane: Are you sure you want to share your money problems? Not sure I can be of any help.

Jill: You don't have to provide me with a solution. All I need is somebody to listen to me.

Jane: OK, go ahead, I am happy to give you a listening ear.

Jill: As I mentioned earlier, I work full time and earn a decent wage. However, I find myself in too much debt and I am always waiting for the pay cheque to come through so I can try and cover my debts. I can't tell you where my money goes to! I don't own a car. I am not paying a mortgage on my house. I am not married and have no children. Currently, I owe the bank $6,000 but just can't explain how I got into so much debt. What do you think?

Since you don't know the extent of Jill's financial history, you find this question difficult to answer, but also saddening.

No matter how much hard she works, it is all futile, since it's likely that she will continue to struggle with organising her finances. So, as a starting point, you suggest that Jill records every dollar she spends so that she has a clear idea about where her money is going.

How can you save money without knowing the overall total record of transactions?

Many people wish to have more money in their bank account, but it seems that the struggle to actually save money is widespread. You might have difficulty figuring out how you can increase the flow of money into your savings account.

Transactions happen every day but whether they meet your objectives in managing money is debatable. Everyone is different in the way they manage their money. There are those who manage their finances according to their needs and others who have no idea what they spend on.

Which group do you belong to?

Regardless of your status, the objective of this book is not to tell anyone how to manage their money, but rather to outline simple, basic steps that facilitate money management.

Many authors have written books on how to manage money and I will not be the last one to emphasise how simple and basic it is to take control of your finances. The language used in this book is straightforward and special care has been taken to eliminate financial jargon and to make the book easy to understand.

Whether you are earning $30,000 or $100,000 in a year, the most important thing is to ensure that you know where your money is spent and to look for ways to organise, save, and enjoy it. A high mathematical skill is not necessary to achieve this, but basic arithmetic is important to recognise the difference between money coming in, money going out and your remaining balance.

Such simple calculations are easily done with a calculator, like the one on your phone. Such everyday technology can eliminate a lot of hassle.

How do you monitor your money?

Below is an example which illustrates how easy it is to organise your finances.

> *A single mother in the developing world wakes up early for one day's work; it might involve working on someone else's land. At the end of the day, she will be paid $20. With such a low income, even relative to the cost of living in her country, the mother will have to manage her money and she has to divide it according to her needs:*

1.	House rent	$5
2.	Food	$3
3.	Cooking oil	$2
4.	Firewood	$3
5.	Children's uniform	$2
6.	Balance	$5

> *which she will keep as savings for a rainy day.*

Budgeting for her needs for her day, she uses simple ways to divide up her earnings and also manages to save a little money for a rainy day.

Now this concept applies to everyone – whether you are in the developing or developed world and whether your income is earned from wages as an employee or money from your own business – the concept remains the same. When managing money, one needs to think smart to stay financially safe and survive.

Contemporary money-spending culture

Most people hear about potential new purchases from friends, work colleagues and relatives in everyday conversation. It may go something like this:

"I have just bought myself a new gold ring, earrings and chain".

"I have just ordered clothes online".

"I am waiting for my new phone to arrive".

'I order five coffees a day'..

"I am meeting a friend for brunch at this cosy restaurant"."We have just put down a mortgage on a new house".

Does this sound familiar?

Yes, these are the things that are done every day and they all cost money. You manage money to make your lives comfortable and provide yourselves with a sense of security. However, it seems that many people spend this well-earned money on what is not needed for a fulfilled life.

Spending money without putting any thought into it leads one to being broke and in debt. You can manage to reduce your expenditure by following simple steps to control your spending. Poor money management is often the result of poor spending strategies. You may find yourself struggling to keep up with an ever-demanding world. You happily spend money using credit cards and forget to keep track of how much is spent.

It is easy to get carried away and buy too many things which you do not need, particularly when using credit cards for shopping. It is worth remembering that this money does not belong to you. It is the bank's money credited to your cards and will have to be paid back to the bank at some point.

How many times have you gone shopping and purchased clothes, got home, tried the items on and decided they were not worth buying or didn't even fit properly? The next step is when those clothes are put in the bin and your money goes into the bin with them. Has this ever happened to you?

Exercise:

Reflecting on managing your money, what strategies do you have in place? List them.

-

-

-

-

-

Section Two

Banks

One thing you may forget is that banks never lose money. They are happy to persuade you to have credit cards and re-assure you that you are well looked after. However, banks are businesses, and like any other business, they have objectives to meet and will never run at a loss. Banks and financial institutions are there to facilitate the offering of loans and financial support.

However, when you make poor financial decisions, such as taking out a loan for a holiday that you cannot afford, the bank will not help you out. You end up creating more issues rather than relieving your initial financial stressors. Hence a responsible approach to borrowing money is essential, and this includes being well informed as to what you are committing to.

Obtaining a loan without a strategic plan in place is a big mistake, as repayment plans can seem reasonable, until payments are demanded every week/month. A bank and its customers have a love-hate relationship – one cannot do without the other.

You need banks to keep your money safe and they rely on you since they utilise your deposited money for their own investments and loans.

Joyce used to receive numerous phone calls enticing her to take up credit cards with her bank. They offered preferential interest rates and all the other benefits that came with those credit cards. After she repeatedly declined their offer, the bank gave up. Joyce realised that she could control how she managed her money. She could limit overspending and live within her means.

The power to manage money can be as easy as A, B, C and D **if you follow basic principles, many of which are presented in this book.**

You don't have to be a financial guru to manage money!

This book explains how you can manage your money. It uses examples based on real life experiences. Managing money starts with small baby steps. It takes discipline, dedication, time and persistence for it to pay off.

Credit vs Debit cards

A credit card is a pre-approved card from the bank which allows you to use the bank's money based on your credit rating or banking history. The money allocated to the credit card is determined by the bank and must be paid back within the stipulated time frame, or on a minimum payment plan. The borrowed money will attract interest if not repaid on time. Credit cards have very high interest rates.

A debit card, on the other hand, is also issued by the bank but in this case the money belongs to the customer. So long as there is money in the debit account there is no limit as to how much you can spend. If the balance in the bank account linked to the card runs out, the card is rendered unusable unless more money is deposited into the account.

Debit cards and the funds within them are easy to manage and prevent over-spending on unnecessary things and the resulting debt. One can still have a credit card and not incur fees in the form of interest by ensuring that the base amount the bank has allocated is topped up; therefore, you use your own money and not the bank's.

In some instances, you might require more money than the topped-up amount on your card and in this case, the bank's money can be used so long as it is replaced before the stipulated time lapses. That way you avoid paying interest.

Credit rating

A credit rating is an assessment carried out by financial institutions to ensure the borrower is capable of repaying loans. The higher the credit rating, the better the chances of obtaining loans. A credit rating is also used to determine the interest rate at which the loan will be required to be paid back.

A credit rating is used as insurance by financial institutions. If the borrower has discrepancies in their record of paying back borrowed money, their chances of gaining future loans are slim.

A credit rating is undertaken by entities separate from the banks or financial institutions (such as a Credit Bureau, or consumer credit reporting agency).

These entities are independent agencies that provide advice on whether a borrower has a history of defaults or has claimed bankruptcy. It is easy to access your credit rating for free and to evaluate where it needs to be improved if you are looking to access loans. Due to credit rating assessments, people who have no loans or debts have a perceived higher risk in securing any loan.

The banks or financial institutions are reluctant to give money in such cases, since there is no history of debt repayment. Even with a clean savings record and the ability to prove that there would be no issues in repaying money, proof of some form of debt repayment is important.

One disadvantage using a debit card is that it does limit the ability to borrow loans from the bank as the bank might decline loan applications if there is no evidence of a credit rating.

To enable you to take out a loan, ownership of a credit card could be of benefit as it can prove that you are capable of repaying the debt without any hassles – essentially improving your credit rating.

Multiple credit cards

Why do you need 4 to 5 credit cards from different banks, meaning that you cannot remember which is which? I recommend consolidating numerous cards into two primary ones and getting rid of the rest. Yes, cut them up and put them in the bin, because multiple cards only create problems for yourself, and make it impossible to manage money.

Having multiple credit cards is different from having numerous bank accounts such as a normal operational account, savings, current and high interest account. Keeping it simple is the key to achieving financial goals.

Key points

- Credit cards incur interest, depending on the bank

- A debit card uses your saved money and no interest is charged for using it

- Ownership of numerous credit cards can create a lot of money-management problems; keep it simple to make tracking your finances possible

- It is possible to use a credit card without incurring interest by either:

1. Topping up and using your own money; or

2. Paying back the debt before the bank's stipulated deadline.

Exercise:

How many credit cards do you have?

-

-

-

-

-

Section Three

Budget

Agreement between partners

Within a relationship, there need to be agreed guidelines as to how the money will be managed, shared and spent. There are no ifs or buts. Trust built through open communication is vital to bring the other party on board for the collaborative management of finances and to achieve financial goals.

Total transparency between partners is important in order to avoid conflict and for the relationship to thrive. Where there is no relationship involved, a single person has the freedom to make their own financial decisions. However, a general principle of money management is to spend 80% of your earnings and save 20%. It is not a perfect ratio but it won't lead to disappointment either.

Managing money using a budget

One simple way to help you manage money: remember that it is hard to get into financial difficulty if you follow this basic principle:

> *The total amount of all expenses should not be more than the total amount of income.*

In other words, you need to spend less than you make. The best way to do this is to develop and use a realistic budget.

Budgets

Many people attempt to create a budget but never keep on top of it. They move off it, relax and revert to their old habits. How many times have you heard your friends say?

"Oh, Jane I tried to stay on top of my money for two months, but found it was too hard and now I find myself in the same position I was in before. I am living from pay cheque to pay cheque! When will this habit come to an end?

The harsh truth is, no-one else can fix your money problems but yourself - by getting your act together and sticking to a realistic budget. Ask yourself, are you one of those who try a budget for a month and then trash it?

Do you really stick to
your budget?

No, I just use the money
as it comes

Exercise:

List the times you have tried to budget and succeeded.

-

-

-

-

-

One obstacle to setting up a budget arises when people think of budgeting as something complicated that requires a high level of mathematical skill. This is just not true; the following explanation indicates how to develop and use budgets and shows that the process is not complicated. It just relies on some self-discipline and the use of realistic figures.

A budget should be a "living document" that is used to compare planned income and expenses against actual income and expenses. It should allow you to make timely adjustments, and avoid financial difficulty. Developing a budget is simple and is made easy by mobile phone and computer budgeting apps – though some of these attract ongoing subscriptions. As the whole concept is to ensure that you do not spend unnecessarily, seek the free budget apps out there.

Alternatively, you can develop your own budget spreadsheet using Microsoft Excel software (Although Excel is not free and has to be purchased to use on computer if it's not already installed.) Either method will require some initial time spent learning how to use the program; but with continuous use, the layout will quickly become familiar.

Generally, each app has its own training guide, so here I will discuss the use of Excel as a budgeting tool, particularly concentrating on the budgeting process and format. Learning resources on how to use formulae in Excel can be easily accessed through Google or other search engines, so I will not explore this. Irrespective of the purpose of the budget, whether it could be to manage the money of a single person, a couple or a family, the same principles and processes need to be followed.

A simple example of a monthly budget format:

Description	Timeframe (weekly, monthly, yearly)					
	Jan	Feb	Mar	Apr	May	June
Income						
Salary						
Grants						
Flower sales						
Total Income						
Expenses						
House rent/mortgage						
Insurance Repairs						
Total Expenses						
Balance						
(total income - total expenses)						

Income includes:

- Wages
- Dividends
- Small side businesses profit
- Gifts
- Interest

  Make sure all income is accounted for.

I am a person who likes to try out different small projects and business ideas. Although these might not produce much income, whatever they do produce makes a positive difference to the achievement of my financial goals.

One recent business endeavour I have explored is making macramé plant hangers and Japanese Kokedama plants which are sold at local markets and online via my Instagram page @jane.kokedamas.

I find making things with my hands therapeutic, and while I enjoy these small projects, a bonus is making a dollar along the way. Some of you undertake side hobbies not particularly to make money but to keep stimulated away from daily work routines. Whatever money you make from your side jobs/ hobbies should be included in you or your family's budget, because budgets include ALL income and expenses.

Expenses include:

- Accommodation (rent/mortgage)
- Amenities (electricity, gas, water, telephone, internet, insurance, furniture, repairs/maintenance)
- Transport (car registration, repairs/maintenance, fuel, insurance, money spent on public transport)
- Personal costs (food, refreshments, gifts, entertainment, recreation, health insurance)
- Education costs – for dependents or university students (school fees, transport, tutors, excursions, uniform, books/ipads/laptops etc…)

    Make sure all expenses are accounted for.

Remember the first suggestion in this book – tracking where your money is going? This is where your hard work comes in handy. Initial figures for expenditure are gained from previously noted costs –for example:

accommodation, school, car, personal recreation.

Tracking expenses

Often personal costs although known, are not linked to specific cost groups. For example, a person often knows that they spend $1,500 per month overall on food, refreshments, gifts, and entertainment, but do not know how much is spent on each item. Breaking down the total figure into how much is spent on each of these items will enable you to better understand how much money is spent and where it is spent.

This allows adjustments to be made if costs increase or income drops. To be clearer on the actual sum spent on these smaller personal items, a record needs to be kept of your spending. Initially this is done daily to get an accurate "average" for the different small item costs. Once this is established, the frequency can be reduced.

You might track personal cost expenses for 2–3 weeks every third month, and this would provide an overview of expenditure on small items over a period of time. This data can be recorded on your mobile phone or simply on a small notebook carried with you.

Another way could be by saving your receipts and checking your bank account at the end of the day, then writing down data from that information. It is a matter of discipline to document the cost of every small item purchased – even a bottle of water, a coffee or chewing gum! Every single item needs to be recorded to present an accurate figure for your budget, which in turn means that your budget will be a better money management tool.

Exercise:

When was the last time you scrutinised your expenses?

-
-
-
-

An example of a hand-written expenditure

17.12.2010.
1) Transport — 9.00
2) Lunch — 7.00
3) Bottled water — 2.50
4) Milk (house) — 2.50
5) Fruits . — 10.00

18.12.2010.
1) Petrol - 30.00
2) Lunch - 7.00
3) Parking fee - 20.00

19.12.2010
1) Household Shopping — 150.00
2) Friday Pie day - 10.00
3) Homeless donation - 10.00
4) Snack Poteto chips — 2.00
5) Coffee x 4 — 20.00

Tracking money

The use of your bank statement to track money

Bank statements are issued every end of the month, usually online, though some people still believe in a printed format where they can track credit/debit card expenses to ensure that balances correlate with expenditure.

This tracking also confirms that the exact amount used is what was deducted. At times it can be difficult to identify whether money is missing if you do not keep an eye on your bank statements. For this reason, it's worth going quickly through them. In this way, bank statements can be used as tool to achieve your objective in tracking your money.

There have also been numerous cases where scammers have stolen credit card details and used money without the owner's knowledge. Having been a victim of credit card theft myself, I know that it is important to go through what was purchased to ensure that you are on top of your money.

If there are any discrepancies or unusual purchases, inform the bank immediately. The banks are aware of scammers and will follow up on these types of cases promptly.

The bank normally recommends cancelling any credit or debit card linked to the scammed account; they will issue a new one and return the money in dispute. There is a risk of time-consuming, constant tracking of money, however making it a habit to do so can lessen feelings of being overwhelmed.

Another way of tracking money coming out of your bank accounts is by listing all organisations which 'direct debit' money automatically from your accounts – maybe for payment of bills and/or subscriptions for some services which you thought were important at the time. Sometimes people pay for services that ceased a long time ago and the organisations were not informed of the changes in your circumstances.

It is not unusual to forget to keep track of all the bills which are paid annually - or sometimes more frequently. In such instances, you should first contact the organisation directly and if they refuse to refund your money, you may lodge a dispute with the bank for the money to be reverted back into your account.

Example: Some years back, Jim was paying for a computer antivirus subscription. However, he had changed to a different provider and had forgotten to communicate this information to the organisation he had subscribed to. Three years down the line, the payment was still coming out of Jim's account. Once he noticed and notified the organisation, they were reluctant to refund the money. The bank was notified, and the money refunded into Jim's account.

How much money goes out of your account that you have no idea about?

Oops
I have quite a few

Exercise:

List all the companies and organisations you have agreements with, and who directly deduct money from your account.

How many have you found and how many of those are you aware of?

-

-

-

-

-

Entertainment money

This is the money allocated within the budget for going out with friends or having a quiet drink at home. Yes, whether alcoholic or non-alcoholic, a drink is important in finding time to reflect on where you have come from and where you are heading.

Entertainment money also includes the money allocated for children's shopping and treats, which we will discuss further later in this book.

Self-treating expenses (essential!)

Although savings are important, life is not all about them and you must enjoy your life and spend that money you work for. A fulfilling and satisfactory life is very important. Therefore, it is essential to look after yourself holistically both mentally and physically, by taking time off work and undertaking those important activities or catching up with friends and/ or families.

Having that special moment to relax provides a chance to adhere to a budget and commit to a long-term financial plan, since life is all about balance.

As an example, my husband and I look for that special moment to entertain ourselves. Even though neither of us is a big spender on social activities, we dedicate time and allocate some money to enable us to have friends come over for lunch or dinner, occasionally go out for a good meal and enjoy the outdoors.

At times we treat ourselves shopping, mostly for the things we need in life and spend money on acquiring a few good quality clothes, shoes or little things that bring joy, like perfume – if one is a fanatic of perfumes like myself. I do love wearing a nice expensive perfume!

Do you have a slot in your budget where you allocate some money for treating yourself?

Budget Outlook Format

As discussed above a budget contains every dollar received or planned for in your money management plan. At first glance you might be surprised with the figures indicated on the tables. However, do not be intimidated as we will cover the aspects of those figures as indicated in the budget on pages 153 and 154.

Comparing actual income and expenses against budget income and expenses.

A budget is a plan and as with any plan, the expected figures for income and expenses can change due to a range of circumstances such as:

- A change to employment
- A change to income from your business
- An unexpected increase or decrease in expenditure
- An unexpected expense arising such as a need to replace a high-cost item. For example, your car may break down and the money saved for a rainy day may not be enough to cover the costs of repair or replacement.

When such a change occurs, it first needs to be identified and then financial adjustments need to be made to cover the variation.

Budget adjustments to be made due to variations in income and expenses

In order to identify if actual income and expenses are varying from the estimated budget, it is important to compare the two sets of figures. If the sum of total expenses is higher than total income, then a person must look at their budget and find ways of adjusting it so that income is higher than expenses by making one of the following choices:

1. Increase income
2. Reduce expenses or
3. A combination of increase in income and reduction in expenses.

The analysis and budget making compared to actual figures.

It is good practice to make these comparisons monthly and assess any variations to allow for timely decisions if required. Using the Budget Tables on pages 153 and 154 as a reference, we will compare the following figures which have been compiled from the month of March.

Table 3: Budget versus Actual for the month of March

Description	Budget	Actual	Variation
Income			
Salary	3,500	3,500	0
Side business	800	500	-300
Interests	200	200	0
Gifts	150	150	0
Dividends			0
Total	**4,650**	**4,350**	**-300**
Expenses			
Rental/Mortgage	1,000	1,000	0
Mobile phone	300	300	0
Utilities			
Electricity			0
Water			0
Gas			0
Purchase new refrigerator		1,200	-1,200
Personal			
Health insurance	200	200	0
Health products	80	70	10
Gifts		50	-50
Food			
Groceries	250	200	50
Lunches	80	120	-40
Transportation			
Car insurance			0
Maintenance/repairs		250	-250
Public transport	200	170	30
Licences road/personal			0
Debts			
Credit card payment			0
Entertainment			
Eating out	100	120	-20
Movie tickets	300	250	50
Sporting events			0
Gymnastics	250	250	0
Beverages	200	150	50
Pets			
Veterinary expenses			0
Food	200	150	50
Savings			
Long term goals	250	250	0
Emergencies	200	200	0
Short term projects	100	100	0
Superannuation/retirement	300	300	0
Total expenses	**4,010**	**5,330**	**-1,320**

Analysis and decision-making process

1. Overall, the variation is that $1,320 more was spent than planned. *If a high variation figure continues each month, expenses across the year will be much higher than income. Therefore, the reason for a higher expenditure than planned needs to be determined.*

2. Looking at the 'variation' column in Table 3 above, the main variation (-$1,200) is for the purchase of a new refrigerator. Comparing this with the yearly budget (page 153), we can see it was planned that this item would be purchased in May. *Since this purchase was planned within the budget there is no need to make any adjustments to the overall budget figures.*

3. This individual's small business suffered a 27% ($300) drop in its expected income. If this continues across the year, there will be a fall in the planned income of $4,013. *The reason for this fall must be identified and a decision made about its continuing.*

Some of the questions to consider are – why is the business not making money? – or evaluate whether the expenses of the business materials are too high hence failing to cover expenditure and make profit.

If the situation looks like continuing then either the business costs need to be adjusted to allow the planned profit to continue, OR budget income and/or expenses items need to be identified that can be adjusted to cover this loss in income to retain the planned budget balance.

Summary: Key points around budgets

- Budgets are only as good as the accuracy of their figures

- Budgets are "living documents" that should be used frequently to compare against real income and expenses

- Regular use of budgets allows for timely decisions to be made that relieve present and future financial pressure

- Making and using a budget is not a complicated process. However, you need serious commitment and discipline to develop realistic budgets and use them regularly

- Finally, if used correctly, budgets are the key to good financial management.

Section Four

Debts

Debt is money borrowed from one party to another through a mutual agreement; this money has a timeline as to when it should be paid back to the owner. An incentive in terms of interest is put on the money borrowed; hence when the debt is paid back the sum is normally higher than the initially borrowed money.

Paying debts

Debt can be annoying and often makes you feel stressed and pressurised. However, it can be easy to stay away from the temptation of being hooked into debt. To keep it simple, there are two different types of debts: good and bad.

Good debt is that which is well controlled, planned and not overwhelming. The borrower can manage their money without putting too much pressure on themselves and negatively impacting their quality of life. A bad debt is one where people impulsively decide to borrow money any time they want for no particular planned reason.

This type of debt can end up getting out of control, negatively impacting your life, and involving a failure to manage your finances.

If you are in debt, listing all your debts would be the ideal way of starting to deal with them. Then, plan for how much money you need to settle that debt within the shortest timespan. Paying off debt quickly saves money by decreasing interest, and it relieves stress in one's life.

To avoid debt, my husband and I ensured that we were not trapped into anything which knowingly or unknowingly would tie us down. Some organisations try and use different tricks to attract people into debt. You should be wary of these.

For example, an organisation approached me with the offer of a very good deal to get a holiday fully paid for if we accepted to pay for two nights with them. The catch was that we could only get this holiday paid for if we agreed to pay a certain amount of money which would be deducted every week for six months and that would guarantee our "free" holiday. While the deal sounded very good at first glance, that free holiday was not free since we were going to permit our money to be deducted automatically from our bank accounts.

Once the contract was signed, that money, although in our bank account was, no longer ours as we had to adhere to the agreed contract. Another condition was to provide the organisation with bank card details even though they had indicated they were not going to deduct money until the contract was signed by both parties.

When questioned further, not much information was forthcoming from this organisation. I instantly declined their offer as we had not planned (budgeted) to go on such a holiday anyway.

The fact remained that this organisation had a drafted policy and in the event that we never read or understood its small-print, we would have blindly committed to pay for a holiday we did not need. Therefore, we find that when the deal is too sweet there is a catch somewhere and you should ask further questions.

How many times have you put yourself into debt you had not planned for?

Exercise:

Write down all your debts and evaluate how well you are doing paying them back. How are you faring?

-

-

-

-

-

Afterpay and other buy-now-pay-later companies

As the name suggests it is paying for goods after acquiring them – essentially a debt.

Afterpay provides the ability to buy something instantly when you do not have money, by enabling later payments in small amounts. It is a great idea but creates unnecessary debt by tempting you to buy spontaneously items that you may not have any need for.

Buy-now-pay-later companies encourage impetuous spending, which can get out of control for people who might have a problem with handling their finances. Similar to sales and flashy marketing, these companies rely on impulsive behaviour to lure you in consuming.

The buy-now-pay-later method takes advantage of your shopping appetite and ensures that people cannot leave the shops-online or in store - without buying goods. The repayment plan after purchasing goods is by directly deducting money from your account every fortnight and paid in four instalments over eight weeks.

While the deal seems good for customers, small companies end up sharing their profit with big companies offering these services.

The popularity of buy-now-pay-later services has increased in Australia; however, it still involves a debt which needs to be paid. Once the agreement has been put in place, you must ensure the account has sufficient money to meet the obligations made before each re-payment date.

Although such payments may initially be interest free, another thing to consider is that if one misses a repayment through lack of finances, the agreement attracts a late fee of $10 and an extra week late repayment attracts $7 – totalling $17 and making the whole point of buying the item at the right price an expensive venture. Another way a late fee is charged due to late repayment is based on the item purchased. If over $40 or above, a 25% of the original order is charged to a maximum of $68 – whichever is higher.

Buy-now-pay-later services such as Afterpay can also have positive outcome if you are able to manage and handle your money according to your plan/budget. At times you might need something that was included in the budget, but for which you currently have no money.

In this case buy-now- pay-later can be of benefit to you, in that you can buy the items required and take the advantage of paying the debt within the given timeframe, so it won't incur any charges. This relieves the financial pressure in the short term while still maintaining your budget as planned. While buy-now-pay-later can be detrimental for some people, it can be used as to advantage by others.

Laybys

Laybys are where you purchase items and enter an agreement on when to pay for those items. The agreement is normally to pay for the goods in several instalments. The difference between Afterpay and laybys is that in the latter case you do not get to take your item home when you purchase it; the shop or vendor keeps it for you until you clear the debt, then the item is released to you.

Depending on the agreement between the consumer and the shop, a cancellation fee might be imposed by the company, particularly if the consumer does not meet their side of the bargain.

The cancellation fee depends on the shop policy. Sometimes consumers could lose all the deposit put down for the intended product. Even though laybys do not attract interest for the items bought, there is still a risk of losing money if circumstances change and one cannot adhere to the agreement.

Another drawback is that the suplier might decide to withdraw from the agreement. Before entering a layby agreement ensure that you read and understand what you are required to do and evaluate whether you can keep that agreement.

Do you really need to put something into a layby?

That is the question you should ask yourself when you go shopping. Follow a process to determine whether you need the intended products.

A process to follow when purchasing could be:

Question 1: "Do I need it?" If the answer is "no" then leave it, simple!

Question 2: "If I need it, can I afford it?"

Question 3: "If I have trouble affording it then what can I adjust to make it affordable?"

The case study below shows how a person can achieve their goals without going into debt. Adjusting one's financial capacity can make a big difference.

Simon needed a new dining table as a replacement for the old one broken beyond repair. After evaluating and undertaking numerous shopping trips he was offered different options to buy the furniture by going into debt.

After deep thinking Simon decided he could not afford a new dining table from the shop, therefore he abandoned the idea of a new table. He evaluated his budget and realised that a second-hand dining table was going to satisfy his needs. He visited St. Vinnies and bought a well-maintained dining table almost 'as new', which fitted his budget and requirements.

Taking advantage of sales

Everyone loves 'sales' as a way of saving money! However, you need to pick the right time to go shopping so that you can save that dollar. Organisations will not have sales unless they can break even, meaning that sales are a bonus and they have already met their target.

The companies elevate their prices during public holidays and those important days when there is a celebration, such as Christmas and Easter. Organisations know for sure that you need to purchase gifts for your loved ones and there is no shortcut due to the importance of the holidays.

Once the 'hype season' is finished you can purchase gifts for the next season at a lower price. Again, it is a 'need versus want' strategy. Otherwise, the concept of saving is invalid, since you are consuming just because of your desire to get a bargain, rather than actually needing things.

Sometimes organisations use the trick of putting up the 'sale' signs since they know it is a sure way of tempting customers to buy their merchandise. However, underneath the sale sign one might find that there is little or no difference between the sale and the original price. It is something you can look for by lifting the price tag to get the original price underneath which ensures that you are getting the bargain as advertised.

Another thing organisations are good at is the use of coupons where you think that you are saving money by getting the prices slashed – in reality this is a trick whereby they use psychological marketing strategies to blind your judgement and excite you to consume more.

Developing your will power and ability to saying NO

Most spending problems stem from the fact that you get attracted to things very quickly and do not think through whether you need those products. Having the will power to take a minute or two and decide whether you require what you want to purchase is a good strategy. Alternatively, another way of resisting temptation is to walk out of the shop, compare prices at other stores and take time out to reflect and make an informed decision.

Are you one of those customers who is easily convinced?

No Money

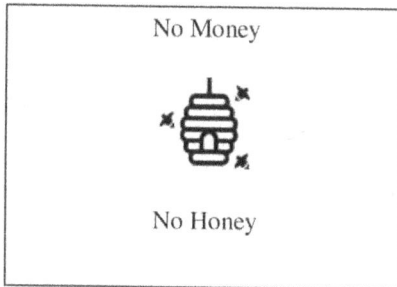

No Honey

Key points about buy-now-pay-later services

- Afterpay and similar buy-now-pay-later schemes are another form of debt which must be re-paid

- If you cannot afford to buy the item in question in cash or have not budgeted for it, ask yourself if you truly need the product by reflecting or stepping out of the shop to give yourself time to think your decision through

- Although these services are marketed as interest free, the products can turn out to be more expensive than initially priced if payments are missed due to low funds

- There can be benefits to using such services, provided you do not over-use them, keep track of repayment dates and aim to pay back borrowed money as soon as possible

- Watch for the right time to buy products and make use of sales to save money.

Exercise:

Can you recall purchasing a product and going into an agreement to pay for it later?

From your experience is it something you would recommend?

What are your thoughts?

-
-
-
-
-

Section Five

Savings

'Savings' indicates the money which is kept aside and not touched unless a very important need arises, or the money set aside for something specific like a car, house or trip overseas. As the saying goes, 'save for a rainy day', because these general savings can come in handy if financial difficulty confronts you or your family.

One example of this would be the COVID-19 pandemic. Unfortunately, many people lost their jobs or faced decreased income and/or hours during this crisis, but those who had some savings put aside were able to use their saved money to survive until they got themselves organised.

Having some savings can provide a safety net for you and your family so that if things get too tough, you could survive for a while without accumulating debt.

Do I need a different account for savings? Ooh yes.

The best option for building your savings is to open another separate bank account and give it the name "savings", or whatever else you decide. Yes, another account different from the one you use every day. This will enable you to stop worrying about saving because every pay day you can organise money to be automatically transferred into that account.

Internet banking is a great way to facilitate automatic transfers – you can channel money into different accounts without any hassles, removing the stress and pressure of doing it manually. Sometimes it can be difficult to have both your spending and savings account at the same bank – especially if you have poor self-control when withdrawing or transferring funds between accounts.

In this case, opening the savings account at another bank would be ideal to remove the temptation. If your financial circumstances change in the future, you may have to re-evaluate the amount of savings going into the account, decreasing or increasing it as needed. However, you should be in it for life-long savings.

Have you tried to put money away just to find you cannot resist consuming it on things you do not need?

Key points

- Create a different account from the normal account and give it a name – this is your savings account

- Budget some money from your pay to go straight to the new account via automatic transfer

- Resist using the money from the savings account.

Savings as an interest earner (making a profit)

Your saved money is your first investment, if used appropriately. Rather than sitting idle in the bank account for the banking corporation to use as investment in their businesses, your savings can earn a few extra dollars. If the bank can make money from your earnings, why shouldn't your money make some profit for you?

The banks often have different savings accounts with different interest rates, and this creates an opportunity to evaluate conditions and choose the best option for your situation. Understanding these interest rates and any other benefits the banks might be offering is important as an investor, since you will gain the skills on how to make a profit by committing to save your money with the offered interest rate.

Alternatively, if empowered with skills, you can decide to move your savings to another bank where interest rates are more attractive. A phone call to the bank is necessary to determine what sort of interest rates the bank offers on the savings account and whether you are getting the best deal.

The use of banking jargon can be confusing, so do not leave the bank or end the phone call without having a good understanding of the products available. This allows you to make an informed decision as to what type of savings account is best for you.

As well as asking your current bank, it is also a good idea to shop around at different banks and compare them. Since interest rates are regulated by the reserve bank, the disparities in interest rate might not be very much; however, even a dollar more in interest would make a difference to your savings. Keeping an eye on your interest rate is vital, due to the failure of some banks to pass on the adjusted interest rates from the reserve bank.

If you are investing your money and the disparity between banks is significant, then it is worth either negotiating with your bank on providing you with a better interest rate or moving to another bank if the money will make a difference to your investment. At times it is good to watch the financial news, since they have updates as such changes develop.

Online financial services platforms

As technology continues to advance, so do online services and financial services. There are now few services which do not have an online banking platform. Some financial services offer their products solely online to attract customers seeking high interest rates. You can save your money with such organisations putting into consideration the risks associated with them.

Like every other investment, the risks of dealing with financial organisations offering online banking services are higher than the normal bank. Money is safer in a traditional bank but good returns are not always guaranteed.

63

As the saying goes, "The higher the risk, the greater the returns".

If the interest rates go up, the total sum of your investment increases; however, should the interest rates fall, then you lose money on the investment, unless you have negotiated a fixed term interest rate. In this case, the outcome of your investment could be higher or lower, depending on the market.

Exercise:

Have a look at your recent bank statements, either on paper or online, and analyse how much interest you have earned per month on your savings account for the last six months.

How well are you doing?

-
-
-
-

Key points on interest rates

- Always shop around for better interest rates
- Follow up on updates about interest rates
- Ask questions to clarify your understanding if unsure of bank terminology and jargon
- Ensure your savings account earns you money through interest. If not, consider making a move
- Compare financial organisations offering online banking services versus traditional banks
- Evaluate benefits and risks associated with financial organisations providing online monetary services
- Interest rates may fall and that will mean lower income from the investment

Fixed interest account

What is a fixed account? A fixed account is where money is put away for a set period of time in return for higher interest. This type of account is suitable for those people who plan to invest their money for a longer period and those who get tempted to use their saved money for unnecessary spending

Fixed account offers options to lock money away for three months up to a year or more, yielding higher returns if the money is locked in for a longer duration. However, I suggest putting money in a fixed account for three months at a time as economic markets change all the time, and it is difficult to negotiate better rates if the money is locked into a long-term fixed account.

However, in the event that you have sufficient savings and no additional money will be needed for sometime, then a long-term fixed account would work and still make good returns.

Evaluate your situation and make an informed decision with your money. As with everything related to investing, there are risks associated with using a fixed account. One of the disadvantages is you cannot remove money before the account matures, which is the agreed time frame with the bank to enable you make a profit.

Another condition is that the customer loses all the interest the account would have earned if they withdraw their money before the maturity date. Taking this into account, a fixed account is not suitable if there is a chance that the money will be needed somewhere else.

Before investing in a fixed account, analyse your financial situation and ensure that you have some money put in a different account to cover you in case of emergency - whether in terms of health, or anything else related to you or your family where you are the only person who can allocate money for emergency use.

Invest and lock some money in a fixed account according to your desired time and make that work for you.

Compound interest investment

When you invest your money into a savings account, you earn interest on that investment. You can choose to use the interest - which is the profit - or otherwise reinvest that money which results in what is called compound interest or compound gains. Your wealth is created from reinvesting interest made from your initial capital investment.

Sue had saved some money for quite some time, and she had no idea what to do with those savings since she had organised her money accordingly for further year. She decided to give a fixed account a go and she locked in her money there for one year.

Once the time elapsed, she had earned some interest on her original money but chose to re-invest that interest back to the fixed account for further year. Her original deposit kept on growing as a result of the additional interest earned along the way. This money she kept on reinvesting is what is referred to as compound interest.

Assume that Sue has $1000 and decides to lock the money into the account for 12 months on a fixed interest rate of 8%. At the end of the 12-month period she will have a total of $1080, with the additional $80 being what she earnt from the interest offered during this time.

If she decides not to remove this money, but to re-invest it for a further year, she will have made $160, assuming that the interest rate stays the same for this period. In a fixed account the interest rate remains the same for the agreed timeframe with the bank. Even if the market becomes volatile, the bank cannot adjust your agreed fixed interest rate.

Key points on fixed account

- In a fixed interest term account money must stay in the account for a stipulated amount of time

- The interest rate is somewhat higher than the normal savings account

- If money is withdrawn before the agreement the client loses all the interest earned

- When the account matures the interest is paid on top of the initial investment fund

- The interest can be reinvested back to the account (for compound gains)

- If money is locked in for a further period, there will be extra earnings depending on the interest rate at the time.

Diversifying your savings

There is a saying that goes "never put all your eggs in one basket" and investments are no exception to this. Diversification is an investment strategy for ensuring that your investments are distributed across different investment portfolios. The importance of diversifying your savings is to ensure that if one part of the market crashes then you do not lose your whole investment, and to reduce your portfolio from exposure to risk and market volatility.

Diversification

Investments range from secure to medium risk and areas of investments could involve financial organisations. Some of these financial organisations are first mortgage services, which I will explain further. First mortgage services are financial real estate investment organisations which are approved and protected by the government– therefore they are legally safe and sound.

First mortgage services offer attractive higher interest rate than the banks. However, the risks are also higher. These organisations require you to deposit money with them and in return they provide you with a list of projects where they invest your money; hence you make decisions based on the portfolio of the projects. Again, you receive your returns every month, even though you can re-invest them in the same projects or identify new ones within the organisation.

For example, if the money invested is $50,000, the company sends out different projects for you to choose from and if you are comfortable with the choice offered, you instruct the organisation how your investment should be divided, according to your desired projects. In the event that you are not comfortable with the identified projects you get in touch with the organisation to ask for different projects until you are satisfied.

For a $50,000 investment you might divide that money into four equal projects with each taking $12,500. This means that your money is safer, in that if one project fails then the rest of the projects may work out as a buffer and you avoid losing all the invested money.

Isn't everything a risk in life? Sometimes you have to take risks to succeed.

Mercy had worked very hard and saved $40,000 within a period of some five years. The interest rates in the banks were once a bit higher at 2.5% and she had been comfortable with the return she was earning. A few months ago, the bank interest rate dropped to 0.80% per annum.

Her money was only going to benefit the bank, since her interest was negligible. Mercy undertook substantial research and found a first mortgage company which offered to give her a 4% interest rate on her money. After the application, the organisation sent out four building projects, each with different interest rates ranging from 3.5% to 4% per annum.

Mercy jumped at the idea and took on the four projects. She is now happily earning better interest on her savings. She is also re-investing her profit with the same organisation.

When we look at Mercy's case, we see that she has managed to achieve three benefits.

1. Mercy diversified her money into four projects
2. She is growing her profits by reinvesting back (compound interest)
3. Mercy's interest rate is better than that offered by the bank, giving her better returns.

Notes from first mortgage investments

- First mortgage investments are protected by the government
- These organisations offer higher interest rates
- Higher risk of losing your investments is involved in investing in these financial organisations than the normal banks
- Interest is paid monthly to a nominated account or can be reinvested back to the account
- Money can be locked into these investments for three years or as per the agreement between customers and the organisations
- No interest is paid at the conclusion of the contract as the interest is paid monthly as per the agreement
- Read carefully any detailed wording of the contract. Ensure you understand what it means and, if you are unsure, seek clarification before signing
- Before investing, make an informed decision.

Exercise:

Have a look at your investment portfolio and see whether you are happy with the extent of your diversification.

Are you benefitting fully from your choice of investments?

-

-

-

-

-

Section Six

Saving for a house deposit

Everyone is interested in having a house to call home. However, houses are not cheap in comparison to the salary most people earn. It takes many years to pay off mortgage debt. A house mortgage is the biggest debt you will ever need to pay off, and there are important points to be considered so you do not burn out or get overwhelmed.

These include calculating the initial payment for the house, the duration of the payment period and understanding how interest rate and other variables (including changes in employment) might affect your ability to cover the payment costs. A lot of people dedicate their lives to paying a mortgage and eventually it is worth having a place to retire in.

For example, a house selling for $500,000 requires $100,000 as a deposit which is 20% of the buying price. A couple with a combined income of $150,000 a year would take approximately 5 years to raise a deposit of this amount depending on their expenses.

Assuming that this couple have other living expenses enabling them to survive, they sacrifice $1,700 per month to save towards the house. In one year, they accumulate $20,400 and in 5 years they will have $102,000 and there is no guarantee that the house prices will remain stable.

There are a lot of proposals from the government, banks and financial services aimed at enticing you to take out a home loan. When you do not have enough deposit even with the help of government funds, it means you will struggle to meet your daily living needs/obligations. It is possible to buy a house if a well-planned strategy is in place to minimise stress related to debt repayment.

There is normally a lot of pressure from friends and family members urging you to buy a house, however, you do not have to please anyone else. You can only do what you think is right for you. To achieve a good house deposit requires opening a new bank account. Yes, another bank account, different from your savings. Give it an appropriate name of your choice.

Allocate a certain amount of money every fortnight to go straight to this account while allowing you to live your lives as normal. Meanwhile, undertake research. Keep an eye on the housing market and how it is performing. When is the right time to commit, there will be enough money to put down as a deposit, and the remaining debt will not be too much to handle.

In times of corona virus, like now, many people have lost their jobs and will be struggling to pay off their mortgage. If house prices go down and the market becomes volatile, this may be a good time to purchase. However, having money in the account could mean the chances of owning a house are higher than if you did not have that money ready.

The downside of having this cash available is that inflation devalues your money and houses might be more expensive than initially thought. There are also options to buy a house with a small deposit and to pay 'interest only' on borrowed money. That means you will not be paying off the house; the only thing you will be paying is the interest incurred on the borrowed money.

For example, if you borrowed $50,000 you will be paying the interest that comes with borrowing this money, but the amount of your debt remains the same.

The interest only payment is only beneficial as a short-term arrangement. Otherwise, it can turn out to be an expensive affair. One is expected to pay the interest and the money borrowed (the principal). The interest only payment can also put the property at a higher risk if the economy is not doing well and house values tumble.

In this case there may be a need to sell due to unavoidable circumstances while the market is down and one cannot make a profit from the investment. However, if the economy is doing well, you have a chance of making money by selling your house.

There are other costs associated with buying a house. Some of these are hidden and not indicated in the selling price, so that you end up spending more money than expected. For example, if the house deposit is less than 20% of the buying price, you have to pay Lenders Mortgage Insurance (LMI).

This type of insurance covers the lenders so that when you fail to meet your side of the bargain, the insurance covers the cost so that the bank or the financial lender does not suffer a loss. If a customer can raise the deposit to 20% then they save themselves from paying the LMI and that money can be used in paying off the house.

Buying a house requires good money preparation to ensure that you can cover all other financial requirements not indicated when the house is advertised. The extras can amount to approximately $30,000 or more. These hidden costs might include:

- Stamp duty (depending on the State in which the purchase is made)
- Mortgage registration
- Transfer fee
- Home contents and building insurance
- Legal conveyancing fee
- Inspection fee
- Mortgage Lending Insurance (if the deposit is less than 20%)

Not enough deposit for the house means bad debt

Mercy and Mary are work colleagues. One lunchtime, the discussion in their office is about where people have invested in their houses. Mercy started the conversation by saying that she and her partner have bought this beautiful house in affluent suburb for $800,000 as their home. Mary also pointed out that she is planning to buy an investment property in another affluent suburb for $1 million.

Another colleague (let's call her Grace) jumped into the conversation and asked both girls how much deposit was required for the houses and both Mercy and Mary replied $40,000.

Mary is already paying a mortgage in the house they are living in. In reality those houses belong to the bank and both families will labour throughout their lives to pay off the mortgages and might never clear the debts.

Assume Mercy's yearly earning is approximately $70,000. After tax she takes home $55,703. If Mercy's partner earns the same amount, their combined income is a total of $111,406 per year. Together, they put down a deposit of $40,000; therefore, they are borrowing $760,000.

After meeting their monthly expenses, they might be required to pay $3,002 per month on an interest rate of 2.5% for 30 years and a fixed term of 2 years where they cannot move from their nominated financier (assuming interest rates remain the same – if interest rates go up their monthly payment will increase).

This repayment covers both interest and principal. Unless this couple has other means of income, it will put a lot of pressure on them as they seek to pay this type of mortgage.

The interest-only scenario

Interest-only loan repayments can be attractive, since they come with lower initial repayments. However, when the loan switches to both principal and interest the repayment increases. Assume Mercy and partner decided to go for an interest-only repayment of $760,000 and put on hold the principal for one year.

The financier agreed to lend them money at an interest rate of 3.5% with loan term of 30 years on condition that for two years they cannot fish for cheaper loans elsewhere. Based on the loan and the interest rate, the couple will be paying $2,227 monthly. However, when interest-only period lapses their loan repayment will jump to a higher amount and this will almost certainly put a strain on their finances.

To avoid stressing about the money, the couple can gradually make extra repayment before the switch. To do this they have to check with their bank on loan terms and conditions. Deciding to buy a house requires a lot of planning and deliberations. So, it is important to consider the risks associated with buying one and have a plan B in place in case things do not go as expected.

The interest rates can be a big determinant of how house markets behave; therefore, having a risk assessment plan in place can ensure that you avoid a nightmare. For example, if there is an increase of interest rates, you will need to be able to cover the discrepancies and adjust to the new rate. The same applies when your income stream changes – as with the arrival of a new baby or termination of employment. These examples are approximations only and do not in any way reflect how organisations charge for their mortgages.

The examples are for educational purposes only. However, make your decisions depending on your own circumstances. Become educated on the mortgage market and its associated risks in case your financial situation changes.

Key points on house deposit

- No concrete deposit means the house will belong to the bank
- Paying for both interest and principal are beneficial to the investor
- Interest-only house payment is only beneficial as a short-term measure
- Risk assessment is important before embarking on house purchase
- Have a plan B in place if situation changes.

Buying a House vs Rental

All people are different and some just want to own their homes without delay – which is good if they have the money to do so. Others want to be patient and build up the 20% deposit so they do not feel overwhelmed with debt. Buying versus renting is a debatable topic but it depends on which side you see yourself on, or what you can afford.

Some people believe that renting is a waste of time, and that money should be put into paying a mortgage. Really? I disagree with that rationale. House renting has its advantages and disadvantages, like everything else in life.

Buying (Advantages)	Disadvantages
• Insurance for the house • Pride of home ownership • Ability to make repairs • Design your house as desired • Can appreciate depending on the economy • No restriction on pets	• Long term mortgage commitment • Not easy to get rid off • Possibility of bad neighbourhood • Patience and time are required when selling • Yearly city council rates

Renting (Advantages)	Disadvantages
• No house insurance for the structure • No yearly city council rates • Freedom to vacate • One does not have to put up with a bad nighbourhood • Repairs are directed to the landlord	• Notice can be given at any time • Non-cooperative landlord • Increase in rent without reasons • Lack of repairs

Even with the disadvantages mentioned above, renting works best for some people. Whether buying or renting, the place you live in is home at that particular time, so make it as comfortable as possible. Treat the house and the compound as your own, and make it feel homely, not just another house.

Rent based on budget

Renting a house is based on an individual's or a couple's income. The renters look around an area that appeals to them and pick out their preferred home. Occasionally, you tend to want to live a life way beyond your means, and as a result find that you are struggling to meet your daily needs due to higher expenses which are not met by your income.

> *Example: You are earning $80,000 before tax, $17,600 goes on tax; the remaining $62,400 is what you take home. You then choose to live in an apartment which costs $2,500 per month; that means $30,000 goes towards the house payment every year and you are left with $32,000. Depending on your needs you might find that the $32,000 cannot enable you to sustain your preferred lifestyle and keep some savings aside.*

Options include renting in a less expensive area, rather than in a first-class environment. In this case the primary thing to do is to make sure it is a safe and agreeable environment for you, your family and your children. This enables you to pay the rent without any hassles, live life to the full and save for the future.

Saving for a trip

A trip is a project by itself, and it should be treated as such. It requires pre-planning and that includes saving money for it. Are you travelling within Australia? Or overseas? Organising for a trip does seem easy since you can get other people (such as travel agencies) to do all the work for you.

Even when using travel agencies, it is still important to undertake some research on the places you intend to visit, to ensure that prices are not too expensive, and find out approximately how much it will cost including air tickets. Sitting down with a travel agent and discussing your interests and your budget plan is important, as is discussing the amount you intend to spend on your holiday.

Take control of your tour travel while taking advice from the tour companies. Also, you may wish to compare what other tour companies are offering for the same services, in order to make informed decisions. Another approach to organising a tour or holiday is to undertake this challenge yourself, without using a travel agency.

It takes a lot of time to organise such trips alone since you need to undertake research, and identify which fares, tours and accommodation suit your budget. If you have the time to research and organise your own holiday trip, you can learn along the way. The internet has provided us all with a platform to undertake research and communicate easily around the world.

Remember, however, that most online platforms offering tour services are third party organisations acting on behalf of the main organisations which provide the services. These third-party organisations are paid by the main organisations if they sell services for them. Dealing directly with the organisations offering services would be the ideal thing to do, even though not always viable.

If circumstances change, the chance of getting a refund is much easier when dealing with the main organisation rather than a third party. In some instances, it is difficult to deal directly with the organisations, particularly when accommodation is involved. In this case, a third party can be useful in booking accommodation. Sometimes it is also safer to use third-party organisations - particularly in securing accommodation - to avoid getting scammed.

However, reading and understanding the small print of any policy is important to avoid disappointment or losing your money altogether.

To make saving for your trip easier for yourself, you can create a travel account, different from other accounts; as discussed earlier, it is easy to create an account online. Once this is set up, you allocate a certain amount of money directly to that account every fortnight from your income.

Forget the account for a while as it accumulates the money. Meanwhile undertake research about your trip and learn more about what interests you, since travelling is more about other people and their history. Some people are interested in birdwatching, yachting and golf tours; whatever tours you choose there is no harm in taking a wider interest in the areas you wish to visit.

Once the money builds up, start paying for the tours, if you have opted to undertake these tasks yourself. Enjoy the challenges as you learn through this experience. By the time the trip is due, there will be enough money to pay for your whole adventure if you have budgeted well. If travelling overseas, just before leaving your home country, ask the bank and the tour agencies about the best travelling Visa card they offer their customers like yourself.

Remember this is your money! The power of negotiation is better than borrowing money. The bank has different types of travel Visa cards, and you have the opportunity to educate yourself about what they entail, and the associated costs. Some travelling credit cards incur a small fee every month but no surcharges on overseas exchange rates.

It is important to let the bank know that you will be leaving the country and for what duration; this ensures the safety of your money. Once you are comfortable with the deal, head off on your trip and have a good life experience.

It is also paramount to ensure that you have internationally recognised currenty in cash, such as US dollars, Euros and/or British pounds. This need not be a large amount – just some money which can be exchanged to local currency at the border/ airport of the international country of arrival.

This is to facilitate payment for small services such as taxis and/ or purchasing telephone start-up cards; sometimes there may not be immediate access to ATMs or credit card facilities. This could leave you vulnerable and insecure in a foreign country.

Exercise

Are you planning to travel soon or later? Challenge yourself, plan organise and research for your tour.

•

•

•

•

•

Travel Insurance

Travelling is fun if all goes according to plan. However, if you are unfortunate enough to experience accidents or illness, and have no travel insurance, the trip could end up costing you and your family a lot of money. Therefore, include travel insurance in your planning, save for it and ensure that you do not leave home without a policy in place.

Travel insurance policies specify what is and is not covered, so make sure you know what you need. It is important to shop around and ensure that you chose a travel insurance which has a good reputation for honouring claims, and can cover your type of travel. Ensure that you read the fine print of the policy, and that you fully understand what you need to do in the event of your making a claim. You would never want to be caught out on your holiday without travel insurance.

Travel account closure

The life cycle of the travel project finishes once the trip is accomplished. Once back home, the first thing is to call the bank to cancel the travel credit cards; their work is finished, and you can save the monthly fees they were incurring.

The next step is to close the travel account, as it is not needed until the next trip project. Any money left from the trip can be put back into the savings account and life goes back to normal.

> *Kelvin decided to challenge himself by planning for a European trip. Once the decision was made, he secured money into a new account and commenced on a journey of saving. Kelvin also dedicated his time to researching the places he wanted to visit, and the accommodation.*
>
> *He secured his accommodation and air tickets with a third-party organisation he found online. It took Kelvin time to come up with an itinerary which fitted his budget, but he enjoyed the experience gained from organising this trip.*

All was well until he commenced his trip, but COVID-19 was declared a pandemic while on his travels and as a result the airlines cancelled his flights back home. Kelvin had a hard time getting his money back as the third-party organisations he used gave him excuses that the airlines had not communicated about cancellation of tickets.

When Kelvin called the airline directly, he was redirected back to the third party he had booked with. Even though he eventually managed to secure his refund, it took him a long time, and unnecessary cost and stress. If Kelvin had booked his air tickets directly with the airline, they would have had no choice but to sort him out rather than push him back to the third party.

Exercise:

Have you ever tried to get your money back after an airline cancellation? How did that go?

-
-
-
-
-

Key points

- Open a trip savings account
- Dedicate some money to be deposited into this account
- Get travel visa cards which will not cost too much in terms of fees
- Consider the international money exchange rate charges, if any
- Acquire a small amount of internationally recognised cash
- Close down the account upon returning home
- Cancel the visa cards when home
- Any money left over from the trip can be put into your savings account or used to fund desired tasks.

Section Seven

Mobile phones on the trip

Mobile phone companies make money through people's lack of understanding of International Roaming fees. When you travel overseas your phones automatically change to roaming services. Due to lack of knowledge, you can be tempted to take the phone International Roaming deal, but it comes with a bitter pill at the end of the trip. The telephone bills will be waiting on your doorstep when you land back home.

I have encountered a few friends who have fallen into this trap, and they could not believe the amount of money they were billed as a result of this simple mistake. This overseas billing is based on those people who are either on phone plans with the telephone companies or post-paid customers.

If you are a pre-paid customer and debt is not in your vocabulary and you refuse to be tied down to mobile phone deals, then the telephone companies won't have a lot of interest in you, giving you the freedom to undertake whatever deal you like for your mobile phone usage.

> *Agnes travelled to Europe, and she was so excited that she could continue using her phone just as she did back home in Australia. She has a monthly plan with one of the telephone companies. What Agnes did not realise is that the roaming fees were very expensive.*

> *A little message popped up on her phone saying she was on a roaming mobile phone but did not take any notice of the charges. Agnes had a great time during her travels, and missed nothing in terms of her communication. When she landed back in Australia her telephone bill was a total shock: she had to settle $3,000 for her use overseas.*

> *Shocked by the revelation, she went to negotiate with her phone service provider to reduce the bill. The company listened to her complaints but said there was nothing they could do to help to reduce the debt. Since she did not have the cash to pay up front, she was put on a plan to settle this unforeseen debt. What a painful lesson Agnes had to learn.*

The best option when travelling overseas is to utilise local sim cards. Once you land in any country your first quest is to buy a pre-paid sim card; these are normally cheap, and often come with some deals. You can also utilise WiFi to access social media appliances even though some caution is needed when accessing sensitive information like bank accounts, due to security issues.

If you do need to access bank accounts, the use of telephone data would be ideal. You might need to call home directly on your overseas phone due to an emergency or other unforeseen reason. In this case there are online platforms where you can communicate for free; however, the recipient must be online to enable you both to communicate.

Where one party is not online but communication is necessary, there are online organisations to whom you can pay a few dollars to provide direct calling service from your mobile phone. These organisations use voice over internet protocol (VOIP) and provide cheap telephone services.

For a small amount - say $10 - you could have 25 to 30 minutes call-time, depending on telephone charges in individual countries. This is a better plan than having a $1,000 bill waiting to be paid for roaming services.

Exercise:

Have you ever fallen into this trap?

If yes, what were the lessons learnt?

If no, then you are now informed and in a better position to handle such cases.

-
-
-
-
-

Key Notes

- Avoid using International Roaming mobile phone offers at all costs

- Acquire a local sim card after landing on the visiting country. Most services are available at the airport

- Use WiFi services to access non- private information where necessary

- Purchase data to access private information such as bank details or transactions

- Keep your normal sim card in a safe place, since you will need it when back home

- Purchase online connections voice over internet protocol (VOIP) services if it is necessary to call home directly to somebody's mobile phone/ or to contact someone who is not online at the same time as yourself.

Saving on mobile phones

Everyone gets excited when a new model or upgrade of a phone comes on to the market. A lot of people get into debt to pay for the new phone which was not in any way on their budget or even on their mind. People forget that once they are hooked up to the phone the debt must be paid – like any other debt.

The phone companies laugh all the way to the bank when they see how easy it is to get people hooked up.

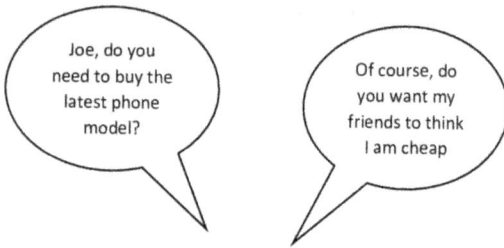

> Joe, do you need to buy the latest phone model?

> Of course, do you want my friends to think I am cheap

However, there are some people who plan to get new phones every time a new one is released on to the market, and this may be alright for them. One of the biggest problems here is dealing with peer pressure and the art of outdoing your friends; yet people can never be equal.

Some people have more spare money than others. Why are you so consumed by what others think of you? Who cares? Getting into debt to please your friends and be among the "well to do people" only contributes to uncertainty in managing your finances.

For that reason, you can buy good phones (but not the latest model) that can deliver the services needed but also stay within your budget. There is no need to stress about new phones since in modern times they only last for two to three years; therefore, a new phone can be in the budget at some point.

What about telephone organisations enticing people with their deals?

Businesses are very clever. They pressure you so you do not necessarily make informed decisions as to what is needed in terms of phone credits, data and the rest. The deal may sound too good to be true, but if you do the calculation, you'll usually see that it works well for the telephone company for you to be on a plan.

For example: A telephone company offers you a new phone, latest model, and it costs $1,500. They talk you into it and the plan gives you a deal paying $90 a month for 24 months. Totalling $2,160.

The deal comes with unlimited phone calls, text messages and 4 GB of data. By the time you finish paying this loan, it will be time for an upgrade for another phone, and the company knows very well that you will be taking up their next proposal. Hence, you become a trapped customer in the telephone industry.

Let's say on the other hand you bought a nice phone for $700 – not the latest model, but good enough to meet all your expectations.

Then, topping up every month with $30 for 24 months will give you 4 GB of data, unlimited phone calls and text messages - all pre-paid. The total will be $1,420 so compared to the $2,160. You save $740! - a bonus you get to keep in your pocket, making you some interest as savings.

The purposes of your mobile phones might be:

- To communicate with your family members and friends

- To take good photos for your social media accounts

- To send messages and receive the same

- To listen to music and podcasts

- To read books online.

Exercise:

Have you ever tried to get out of the telephone plan? If yes, how did you go?

-

-

-

-

Other areas in which to save money

Many people leave the lights on in their home most of the time; sometimes they do not even realise this, or remember which lights are on. These lights consume a lot of electricity which results in an increase in bills. The same applies to wall switches - normally they are left on even when nothing is attached to them. Televisions are left to run all day long even when there is no-one in the sitting/lounge room.

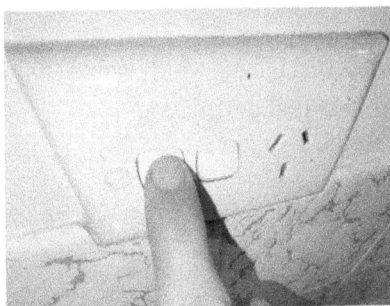

Does this sound familiar? Well, it might seem nothing but if you turn these gadgets off, you can compare the difference in the bills. By doing this you're able to check how many kilowatts are used per hour when the lights are left on. Then turn the switches off, and in the next bill check how much less has been charged for the energy use.

Other ways of saving energy within your home include Low Energy (LED) bulbs. These bulbs consume very little energy and last longer. In Australia we are fortunate in that the government provides these bulbs once in a while. When this project comes up, you and your family may be eligible to receive these bulbs at no cost. The government normally runs these projects every two to three years.

Other small but applicable ways you can save money are by not leaving heaters on when not in the room or adjusting and cooling temperatures, so they are not too hot or too cold. Saving energy also contributes to a better environment, since here in Australia most energy is obtained from coal. If every one of us saved energy there would be less coal mining which would in turn help to reduce environmental destruction.

Fast food and saving by cooking (market or supermarket)

Do you like cooking a good meal and enjoy working with your hands? Cooking good food is an art and it is also therapeutic, there are a lot of good cookbooks, and the internet is full of endless cooking recipes. However, you still find that fast food is consumed in some homes since it is 'cheaper'.

Yes, it is cheap at the point of consumption but not cheap when one is fighting diabetes, obesity, and other lifestyle related diseases due to poor food choices.

In fact, fast food is not always cheap when you do the calculation for what you purchase. Let us assume that three days each week you order food from outside - the food also includes a delivery fee if you are a family of 5 people; the food might cost $10 per person, which is $50 all up plus the delivery fee of $5, making it a total of $55. Multiply that by 3 days. Total of $165.

That's a lot of money for a family of 5, which you could put towards fresh ingredients and using your kitchen to produce an economical and healthy meal.

If you put the $55 into buying food and cooking for one day this is what you might end up having:

1. Get to the market and buy two chicken breasts $5

2. A packet of dry lentils $5

3. Tomatoes $4

4. Some unions $4

5. A packet of brown rice $5

In total you have spent $23 on a healthy lentil and chicken casserole.

The balance can put towards another day's meal, and eventually money will be saved. This does not mean to say that the family cannot occasionally treat themselves to a fast-food meal. However, that should not be an everyday routine.

Even with a small garden you can manage to grow some vegetables such as broccoli, kale, cauliflower, silver beet and blueberries. Herbs are easy to grow and can be harvested, dried and used for seasoning. Most of these greens can be grown in pots (yes pots!) and the results are amazing.

Growing your own vegetables, then eating them after your own hard work, gives great satisfaction.

A blueberry shrub which produces good quality, tasty berries.

Exercise:

Do you prefer to cook a good meal or eat out more often?

-

-

-

-

Key Notes:

- Dining out occasionally is sociable and healthy
- Cooking your own food encourages healthy eating
- Growing vegetables is therapeutic and saves money
- Visiting markets helps you to interact with people and support local farmers

Doing away with pleasing family and friends

'Living beyond your means' is the order of the day in some families. This is contributed to by pressure from families, work colleagues and friends.

There is a notion that one must live in an affluent suburb, go for brunch on weekends, and have gourmet food and coffee; otherwise, one cannot fit in with some social circles.

Who cares where you live and what you eat?

When you place too much importance on what other people think of you, rather than thinking for yourself, you lose the value of living. All you do is to incur debt so that your families, friends and colleagues can see that you are doing 'alright', even when underneath there is a pile of debt and doubt.

Valuable friends do not judge you by what you can afford or your lifestyle; they are there for you irrespective of your financial background.

John and Jacque both completed medical school and got married soon after their studies. They realised that all their friends had bought houses in the upper portion of the property market. Since they were both doctors, they felt they should aspire to live in an elite suburb.

However, John and Jacque were still juniors in their roles and therefore struggling to live a lifestyle beyond their income. Due to peer pressure they both entered the world of debt where they had to pay off a large mortgage, vehicles and live a lifestyle deemed suitable for doctors.

Well into their careers and lives, with children on the way, they were still struggling to pay off debt, but just managing. John worked long hours and undertook some consultancy work to make more money to keep the family going.

Later, John realised that he didn't have a warm relationship with Jacque as they had grown apart while chasing the money; furthermore, the children had little contact with their parents due to the adults' busy lifestyles. Time is important, and spending time with loved ones is worth more than gold. It's possible to chase money and forget to live your life.

Section Eight

Superannuation or retirement savings

This is a regular payment made by your employer towards a future pension, which means that while you are employed this money is put aside in a preferred superannuation fund organisation. You cannot access this money until the time stipulated by the government. However, if you are not a citizen or permanent holder or has no intention of living in Australia after your period of work then you can get access to your superannuation.

It is deemed by law that an employer must contribute to an employee's superannuation fund; at present they must contribute 9.5% of any income incurred including bonuses, commissions and loading. This is called a "super guarantee". This proportion rose to 10% July 2021 and will increase 0.5% each year till it reaches 12% in 2025.

People move between jobs all the time, and often forget to change their superannuation organisation funds. In this case workers accumulate multiple superannuation fund organisations. When you join an organisation there is lack of education on superannuation; however, your employer might ask whether you have a superannuation preference, if not, they put your money directly into their super organisation.

What you fail to realise is that every superannuation fund organisation managing your money imposes administration fees which are deducted from your money. Therefore, instead of some of this money going into your future savings, it is wasted in fee payments. In some cases, you tend to ignore or fail to understand that superannuation is your money. Some people even assume it is a government project.

If you happen to have multiple superannuation accounts, the best thing to do is to choose one consolidate them into that. You need to communicate to the other organisations informing them your intention to transfer your money to the allocated superannuation organisation. Undertake the paperwork/phone calls/online forms required, and the organisations will ensure that your money is transferred to where you require it to be held.

When joining a new organisation, the best option is to provide your employer with details of your existing super fund organisation and your money will go directly to your choice of organisation. This will minimise the pain of dealing with many superannuation organisations, and keep your savings together, with a single fee charge.

With superannuation, you should shop around and do a lot of research on different organisations, their administration fees and what other incentives they offer to manage your money.

I have worked alongside colleagues who had no idea how much super they had accumulated over their years of work, which is a serious misunderstanding of what superannuation is about. One of my workmates said that super is "not his money so why would he be bothered following it up?" Sad but true. What you need to know is that when you retire this money becomes very important in your lives.

The government has just announced that changes to superannuation will be coming into effect soon. All employees will have only one organisation to manage their money rather than getting a new superannuation organisation every time they move jobs. This initiative will save a lot of employees who struggle to manage their super if it is held by multiple organisations.

Superannuation needs to be paid whether you are working full-time, part-time, or casually. Another legislation that may also be coming into effect is that every employer will be obliged to pay superannuation, even when an employee has not earned $450 per month. It is important to be educated concerning your superannuation and be empowered as to what you can and cannot do with your money.

Exercise:

Have you been on top of your super?

-

-

-

-

-

Investing or topping-up superannuation

Would you like to enjoy a decent retirement? For most people the answer would be a yes. However, nothing comes easy, and the more you put to your super the better it is, and the more comfortable your life becomes when retired. Topping up your superannuation can be done after you receive your salary, by allocating a little bit of money, $30 per week, to automatically go through to your chosen superannuation organisation. This will all add up over the years. Another way to increase superannuation savings is by undertaking super sacrifice.

Super Sacrifice

What does it mean to super sacrifice your income?

Super sacrifice is when you choose to put some of your pre-tax income into superannuation, which means that while the money you take home is a little bit less, you are building towards your retirement savings. On top of super sacrificing, the employer must contribute their 9.5% as required by the law. Super sacrifice benefits both the employee and the employer, since it is taxed at a flat rate of 15% up to $25,000. Anything above this amount is taxed at 30%.

To benefit from this scheme:

- You should ensure that your organisation offers super salary sacrifice options and take advantage of that

- Communicate in writing and secure a written agreement on how much you are intending to contribute and how often

- Ensure that money is deposited into the nominated superannuation account and counter check your payslip to make sure they correlate.

Contribution after tax

Some people do not undertake super sacrifice but make superannuation contribution after tax. In this case the government offers an incentive for those who earn less than $54,837 per annum. If you contribute to your superannuation after tax, you might be eligible for a government co-contribution.

This scheme enables the government to match 50 cents of every dollar contributed to superannuation after tax up to a maximum of $500 per year. Therefore, if you want to get $500 co-contribution from the government you have to put in at least $1000 and be within the required salary threshold.

Annie was working in a hospitality industry where she earned $40,000 per year. She decided to put some money into her superannuation after tax and within one financial year she had contributed a total of $1,000

Annie applied for the government co-contribution scheme where she qualified to be a beneficiary and therefore the government paid $500 into her superannuation account. Annie's contribution that year was increased by $500. This money was paid directly into Annie's superannuation account after she submitted her tax return.

You may be able to claim a tax deduction at the end of the tax financial year on the money contributed after-tax income; however, this money has to come directly from your bank account and straight into your superannuation fund organisation. To enable this to happen, a written communication to your super fund organisation is a must.

You submit a form called Notice of intent to claim or vary a deduction for personal contributions (NAT71121) and your super fund organisation must acknowledge your intention. Communicate with your tax return agent and find out what you can or cannot do.

Also, you can find information on the government tax website. It's worth taking the time to read it. Certain people might not know about some of this information and therefore it is important to keep up to date with government policies – they change all the time, and some can be beneficial to your finances.

Alternatively, take every opportunity to learn from your superannuation organisation about what you can do with super contribution.

Keep an eye on your superannuation account

To ensure that your money is going to the right superannuation fund organisation, your first step is to check your payslips and confirm that the money has been paid to the nominated organisation. The next step is to set up an online access account with your superannuation organisation and have log-in details.

Once logged into your account, go through your statement to view your employer's contributions and compare them to your payslips. Any query or doubts can be directed to your employer. Some employers do not submit their contribution immediately and it might take three or so months. It is imperative to know when your employer submits your superannuation contribution, to avoid conflict.

Superannuation funds are also invested into different investment portfolios by the superannuation organisations, so as a contributor you can request where you want your money to be invested.

Most of the superannuation funds invest into share markets, property markets and high or low risk money markets. This is diversified to minimise the risk of investment loss. It is worth following up on how your superannuation funds are performing through the nominated superannuation organisation.

Happy savings in your superannuation:-)

Exercise:

When did you last keep an eye on your superannuation?

Spare a few minutes and check through your payslips and superannuation account.

-
-
-
-

Key points to superannuation

- Superannuation is an entitlement of an employee and is paid by the employer

- Money from superannuation cannot be withdrawn until the stipulated age

- An employer is obliged to ensure that this money is paid to a nominated superannuation organisation

- 9.5% is what the employers are supposed to contribute, provided the employee has earned $450 per month (though the $450 requirement will cease from the 2021-22 financial year)

- Consolidate super to avoid paying extra administration fees to multiple organisations

- The new changes will be beneficial to employees managing their super from one organisation, rather than multiple sources

- Superannuation is invested into different share markets; however, the interest is re-invested back into your superannuation.

Salary sacrifice or salary packaging

Salary sacrifice is a scheme where one can reduce the amount of tax paid on one's income. This scheme is only available with some organisations - mostly not-for-profit organisations. Salary sacrifice is where one arranges to receive less income after tax. In return, the employer pays for pre-tax salary benefits, such as a car, telephone, payment of rent, electricity or utility bills. However, it is important to check with your organisation on what things can be salary sacrificed.

An example of how salary sacrifice works:

> *Assume Alexandria's salary is $90,000 per year and she opts to salary sacrifice for her house rent which amounts to $15,000. Therefore, her take home salary will be $75,000. So, instead of Alexandria paying tax on $90,000 income is taxed at $75,000 which means her tax is less by 15,000 which is a benefit to her.*

Some salary sacrifice is organised by other organisations rather than one's own employer. It is important to find out which salary sacrifice organisations are affiliated with your employer and acquire information on how they go about it. The benefits of salary sacrifice are immediate, while in super they are realised later in life.

All in all, both are designed to save some money for you. Salary sacrifice can be very confusing to a lot of people, and I was no different. However, since I am a persistent person, I took the initiative, undertook research and got education from the organisations which offered salary sacrifice programs.

Exercise:

Can you now tell the difference between super and salary sacrifice?

-

-

-

-

-

Buying a car

New vehicles are enticing, and the urge to buy one is tempting. However, to buy a new car you must have the money at hand or take a loan to pay off the vehicle. Do you really need a loan to buy a car? The answer for some people would be no, for others it would be yes. Even though the desire is to have a new car, if there is no money to afford one then an alternative should be sought.

Buying a recent model second-hand car which you can afford to pay for up-front can be rewarding, and reduce the stress associated with finance. You might prefer to share one vehicle between partners to avoid the expenses associated with managing more vehicles-such as road registration, insurance and maintenance fees.

However, as needs can change and there may be difficulty getting to work, some families may have no choice but to purchase another vehicle. Some people would prefer to purchase a new vehicle outright, with zero kilometres on the odometer. In this case, taking it on as a project would be the safe way to raise money to achieve this objective.

Opening an account to accomplish this wish is a good idea; allocating money to go into this account and putting a time frame on when the goal will be achieved will also be helpful. When all this is in place, the last part will be to undertake research about suitable vehicles for your family, environmental impacts, and bargains available when the time is ripe to buy your car.

This strategy avoids paying interest over the time the car will be paid off. It also takes a burden off you to be debt free and provides you with the freedom to sell the vehicle without clearing the sale with the bank – should the need arise. If you are working in the city and public transport is available, money could be saved by parking for free at a suburban station and part-commuting the rest of the way to the city; this could be the cheapest way to commute to work.

Not a perfect solution, as public transport has its own problems; also, parking can itself be a problem and might be expensive. The use of public transport does not only facilitate saving some extra cash but saves you the time and headache of looking for parking. If you're tired from work and driving home in traffic, there is a risk of having a road traffic accident. To avoid this, take a nap in the train and set a timer on your phone for your train station destination, to avoid being carried past your stop.

Margaret is a young lady who just completed her nursing degree. She is lucky enough to have secured herself a job and soon she will be starting work. She has an old car which was given to her by her parents after completing high school and now she feels that she needs a brand-new car. She had saved 10,000 dollars and after researching new cars the one she is interested in costs $25,000.

Margaret visited the bank for a personal loan, and was told they could provide her with one but she would have to pay an interest rate of 3.97% p.a. on it. After undertaking more research, she found a similar car with 10,000-kilometer reading, well-kept and clean. The car was priced at $11,500, and with $10,000 at hand she only has to raise $1,500 and she will have her car – not new, but in good order. What do you think Margaret should do?

If Margaret decides to go with plan A and borrow the money from the bank, the car will cost more money than initially thought, since the interest rate has to be paid back to the bank and the car will lose its value.

The best plan for Margaret is to go with plan B – to borrow $1,500 from her parents, purchase a second-hand car, and own it outright with no debt to pay. She can then look forward to starting her career without any debt and continue to build her future.

Car Wash

Most roads are well maintained with little dust, so less car washing is required. While it is good to keep the car clean and well groomed, you can undertake this task by yourself and spend time cleaning your car occassionally, when needed. Washing your own car enables you to connect to it and get to know it well, and is good exercise.

At times a serious car wash might be necessary, and this cost can be put into consideration when allocating planned expenditure. It might not seem that you would save a lot of money by washing your own car, but you would be surprised how much it adds up over time.

Car Insurance

Insurance is a big part of our lives, and you cannot afford to drive your vehicle without having insurance in place. There is a saying that if you cannot afford an insurance, you cannot afford to have a car; it is an absolute necessity. To insurance companies, car insurance is a big business and there are a lot of products out there.

The main aim of having insurance is to ensure that if you have an accident, you can be compensated for it. The other benefit of having a car insurance is to ensure that the other driver is similarly compensated. Sometimes people are not able to afford comprehensive insurance; however, third-party insurance covers any damage to the other cars in case of an incident.

Every year the car value depreciates but the insurance premium for the same vehicle increases. Insurance companies can promise a lot of good returns but as a customer it is your work to find out what these companies offer and shop around for better deals. Sometimes you can be stuck with an insurance company for a very long time by being loyal, so it is important to apply bargaining strategies when renewing the cover; otherwise look around for a better deal. There is no obligation to be stuck with one insurance company.

Joan bought a car and purchased insurance from company A for 5 years. Once COVID-19 knocked on the door, the car was not driven very much and was parked on the driveway most of the time during lockdown.

The renewal advice came in around at the usual time and the quote was $1,300 for comprehensive insurance. Joan tried to bargain for a reduction of the premium since she had been along-time customer, but the company would only deduct $5, bringing the premium down to $1,295.

Joan promised to pay the insurance nearer the renewal date. Meanwhile, she decided to call other insurance companies and found one which was offering the same coverage for $1,020. She took that opportunity, paid for her insurance with the new company and saved $280 which she put to another use. Sometimes shopping around can make a slight difference.

Health Insurance

Health care insurance is also important for your well-being. In Australia we are lucky enough to have the Medicare healthcare system in place. Having private health insurance is an option, since it offers a range of services such as having more prompt access to surgery in private hospitals rather than having to wait for the public system. For high income earners, paying for healthcare insurance is an incentive to tax deduction, otherwise you pay a higher rate on the Medicare levy.

However, in the event that you are short of finances and cannot afford health care insurance, you can still access treatment through the public health system. Again, if looking for a good health care package shopping around would be ideal, and it's important to read the small-print information about what the insurance companies are offering to their customers.

Happy insurance shopping :-)

Exercise:

Reflect back on your insurance policies. When did you last change insurance companies?

•

•

•

•

•

Section Nine

Shares

Introduction to shares

Any investment is a risk and shares are no different. Shares are affected by economic and situational changes within countries and across the world. These changes can quickly raise or drop share prices, often affecting different shares in opposite ways. This can be seen with the tour and travel industry share market, including airlines, due to the COVID-19 pandemic, which changed the way markets operate throughout the world.

If you had invested your savings into shares in the aviation industry you could be struggling or even going into a loss, since most airlines made little profit once they grounded their flights. Other flights are operating at a minimal rate; airline tickets are expensive and hence not many people can afford them. The reality of any market is that it can be volatile, and the share market is no different.

The advantage of shares is that as a long-term investment you can leave your money there until the market picks up and share prices go up again. The whole concept of shares involves taking a gamble – by buying, you hope that shares will rise, grow and make money. However, as with the aviation example, shares can lose value abruptly and that means your money also goes down with the organisation. The key to shares is knowing when to buy and the right time to sell.

Investing in shares

There is information available on share investments; however, there is little education on what shares actually are and how one can invest in them. At times there is a lot of discussion of share markets and shareholding, but plain language is seldom used to enable an ordinary person to understand the system. It takes a lot of reading and going to seminars to understand how shares work and with the advent of COVID-19 many people are using Facetime to do this. Even with all this information available, the way shares work is still not very well understood by most people.

How do shares work?

This is how shares work. As an individual it is impossible to operate alone – a third party is required to undertake this role. Therefore, a broker who is authorised to work with the Australian Securities Exchange (ASX) is the ideal person to take on this role.

Once a broker is identified, you chose your shares wisely relying on companies' history and their performances. The next step is to create an account and buy shares. Most banks have a brokerage department which deals with shares, but there are other companies which offer the same services. It doesn't hurt to shop around for better deals as these companies charge fees for their services.

The following page has an illustration explaining the process of buying and selling shares.

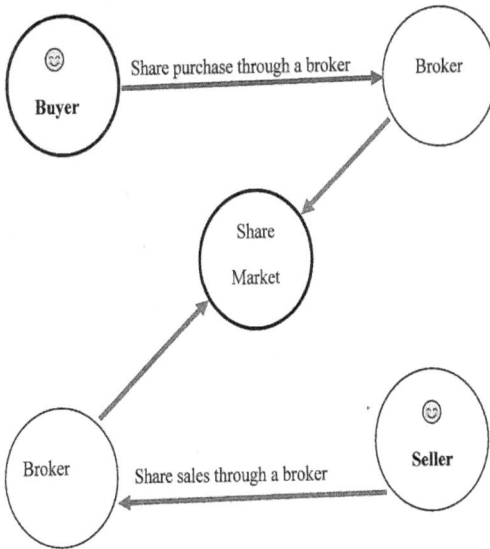

'Brokers' activities are not just limited to the Australian market. Diversifying outside the country is also an option and some brokers are participants in share markets overseas. When investing outside the country it is important to consider the exchange rate between currencies. If your currency is weak against other major currencies, that means that buying shares will cost a little bit more after conversion.

Shares at a glance

In simple terms, shares are like having different types of food on one plate shared among different people. Shares simply mean the ability to own a part of the company by buying some units. These units are managed through stock exchange–markets where buying and selling take place.

Shares are like this food, which is shared among a few people

For instance, company A has a stock price of $40 per share and you invest $3,000. That translates to 75 shares. Let's assume your money has been in the company for several years and the performance has shown consistent growth. Since you own part of that company, you too get good returns.

If the stocks rise to $80 per share the value of your investment would also rise, meaning that you could make a profit by selling one share for $80 and making a profit of $40 per share depending on the number of shares initially invested.

While shares can make a profit for you, they can also do the opposite. If a company you invested in is not performing well and the returns are negative, you make no money and go at a loss. When organisations have a productive year and make a profit, they might share it with their shareholders and this profit is called dividends.

Key notes on shares

- They are not a quick money-making investment

- Always better as long-term investments

- They may earn dividends along the way as shares continue to grow

- One cannot buy or sell shares directly from the market – a broker is always needed

- The global economy and politics can affect the Market.

There are different types of shares, such as ordinary, preference, company-issued and speculative stock, among others.

Ordinary shares

'Ordinary' refers to the common shares which represent normal equity ownership in a company. These shares allow a shareholder to vote, receive dividends and receive distributions in case a company shuts down. However, the payment of dividends is at the discretion of the company.

For example, if a company does not make enough profit over a given period of time, they might decide not to pass whatever profit they make to their shareholders. The company can only share what they make as a profit with their shareholders.

The ordinary shareholders receive information about the organisation's performance and are invited to attend their annual general meeting. The shareholders are involved in the decision making of the organisation when they are given a chance to vote on different issues raised. In this case, shareholders can be voted onto the organisation's board, and have a say in the management of the said organisation.

Jack and Kim decided to invest some of their money into a shareholding market; they signed up and chose ordinary shares as their preference. The couple bought some few thousand dollars-worth of shares.

While purchasing those shares, they decided to split them into different companies to minimise chances of losing a lot of money in case the organisations went broke. In their portfolio they had three companies all well- known and with high ratings.

For the first few years, Jack and Kim received dividends along the way after every three months and they reinvested it back into shares. It was all going well until COVID-19 knocked on their doors and no dividends came their way since the companies they had invested in had lost a lot of business.

However, their shares are still safe since the companies are still in existence. Once the business go back to normality and make some profit, Jack and Kim might continue to receive their dividends and the share prices could go up, which might increase their capital investment.

Preference shares

Preference shares, as the name indicates, provide preferences to their shareholders. For example, the shareholders might get a fixed dividends payment or if a company goes into liquidation (bringing a business into an end, when the assets are distributed to their owners), the shareholders get priority rights to be repaid.

The fixed dividends provide the preference shareholders with certainty over their investment as they receive their dividends before the ordinary shareholders receive theirs. Preference shareholders do not have the right to vote or make decisions on behalf of the company like the ordinary shareholders.

Therefore, preference shareholders cannot influence the company's decision making. One of the disadvantages of having preference shareholding is that you have little influence on the policy making of the organisation. However, your investment incurs a low risk.

Speculation stock

Speculation stock is based on speculating when prices might go up. As the name indicates, this form of investing resembles a form of gambling where no-one can be certain which direction the shares might take.

The investor invests their money by buying shares at a low price, judging that in the near future the prices will go up and that re-selling the shares will make a profit. It is a short- term type of investment, and you need to be connected to the market to make the right decision at the right time.

It is also a high-risk investment. Before investing in shares, ensure that you undertake enough research and education to understand fully how the share market works and which shares best suit you.

An alternative is to hire a person who is fully conversant with how share markets perform, to educate you. One of the key components in share market research is to look at financial performance through yearly financial reports.

Investing in shares and leaving the money to perform without any follow-up is not good enough. As with everything else, some research is important so that you can assure yourself that money is not going to be wasted. Investing in shares is like putting money into any other investments.

At times organisations don't perform exceptionally well for a long time and hence keeping an eye on the performance of those shares is important. However, one does not engage in shareholding with the expectation of a quick return on one's money; it takes time. This is not a get-rich-quick scheme.

Selling of shares

Decisions about selling shares come from the investor and are made after undertaking research and realising that either:

- The company the shares are invested in has not been performing well for quite some time

- The shares have made a satisfactory profit and you would like to get rid of some of them and leave others

- The shares have made a good profit and the investor is not interested in keeping them

The investor alerts the broker and advises which shares they would like to sell. Getting rid of underperforming shares is acceptable and in fact is the right thing to do, before the investor starts losing the initial investment capital. There is no point in holding on to underperforming shares, particularly if one has had them for a long period of time.

This got me thinking.

Bonds

Bonds are more like shares for medium to long term investments. They are also managed by ASX where brokers are involved in buying and selling. However, bonds are seen as less risky than shares and property investments. When you invest in bonds, you are lending your money to a company or government at a fixed interest rate.

Of course, government bonds are safer than those of private companies, which carry a higher risk. In return for lending your money through bonds, you receive regular interest payments at different intervals over the life of the bonds. These are called coupon payments and can be part of your income.

In case you hold the bond until it matures (at a confirmed date when you receive your investment back) then you get the face value of that bond. The face value (or par value) is the money paid to a bond investor at the maturity date provided the investor did not default on the agreement. Therefore, you receive the face value plus the interest (known in bonds as 'coupon payment') at the time of maturity.

However, bonds can be affected by changes to interest rates. If interest rates are falling, the bond prices rise, however their yield falls.

In fact, bonds do not have a standard interest rate but two components: the yield to maturity and the coupon interest rate. The yield to maturity is the total income anticipated at the maturity of a bond. There are two different bonds in Australia: Exchange-traded Treasury Bonds and Exchange- traded Treasury Indexed Bonds.

Exchange-traded Treasury Bonds (eTBs)

Exchange-traded Treasury Bonds (eTBS) range from medium to long term debt securities and pay an annual fixed interest rate over the life of the security. The earnings are paid at an interval of six months. It is one of the low-risk investments with secure earning over the period of the investment. These bonds have a fixed face value of $100 for the life of the securities. The market price of eTBs is more stable than that of normal shares.

Katie decided to invest in government bonds and put a $100 as her investment capital. The bond offered 6% per year on a fixed coupon interest rate. Therefore, Katie will receive 3% after six months and another 3% at the end of 12 months. If Katie was to invest in this bond for 5 years the coupon interest rate of 6% would be paid yearly at an interval of six months.

At the end of her bond investment, Katie will have her $100 back plus the 3% coupon interest upon the maturity of her investment.

Therefore in 5 years, Katie will have $30 as profit plus the initial capital she put into the investment.

Exchange-traded Treasury Indexed bonds (eTIBs)

This is one of the most secure investments and does not have a fixed face value. The face value of these bonds gets adjusted according to the Consumer Price Index (CPI). This means that inflation does not affect the investment and the investor does not lose money as a result of it. Their coupon payment is paid at an interval of three months.

Investors require a CHESS (Clearing House Electronic Sub-Register System) account which records shareholders to enable transactions. Your stockbroker can facilitate accessing CHESS account.

Stocks versus bonds?

Well, bonds come with fixed interest rates that promise a certain return, while stocks have a degree of unpredictability, depending on the market. Which one is better?

Before investing in any form of shares or bonds, you need a lot of education from a financial advisor or shareholding broker to enable informed decisions.

Exercise:

Did you ever believe there were so many different channels through which you could invest your money?

-

-

-

-

-

Types of investments: risks returns versus risks

Investments	Returns	Risks
Ordinary Shares	• Depend on performance of the companies • Stable political and economic situation can result in good returns • Dividends are paid at regular intervals	• Investor can lose it all, including the capital • Can be volatile; local and international markets can change the performance of the specific market
Preference Shares	• Safe investment • Fixed interest rate Shareholders are prioritised	• Share prices fall when interest rates go higher • Call risk (companies can redeem shares when needed) • Lack of diversification
Speculation	• Like gambling, can make money quickly • Depends purely on luck (or judgement)	• Higher risks due to changing of the stock market • Not a long-term investment • Can lose money quickly

Exchange -Traded Treasury Bonds(eTBs)	• Interest in fixed amount • Coupon payment (as profit) • Stable market price • Guaranteed returns –mostly with government bonds	• Low risk • Investing in Corporates
Exchange Traded Treasury Indexed Bonds (eTIBs)	• Interest rates payable every three months on the life of investments • Investment is protected from inflation	• Raising interest rates can translate to falling of eTIBs price • A decline in the consumer price index affects coupon interest payments and the nominal value payable at the time of maturity can decline

Exchange Traded Funds known as ETFs

Exchange-traded Funds (ETFs) are security funds put together and trades like stocks. ETFs pull money together from different investments such as stocks, bonds and other securities, put them into one basket and spread the funds to different securities, hence providing the investor with diversification.

The diversification involved in ETFs can help minimise risk in investments. Therefore, ETFs provide the opportunity to participate in multiple purchases of securities with only one single purchase ETF.

EFTs are also traded on a stock exchange, bought and sold like stocks. However, ETFs incur commission and other related fees just as stocks do. They are purchased through a broker and traded throughout the day, unlike stocks.

There are a variety of different ETFs, each with different objectives. Some ETFs might invest in a variety of stocks and bonds, others in particular market such as health, pharmaceuticals or technology.

Return on ETFs

ETFs work the same way as shares. There are two ways in earning on your investments – by the value of the investment's price going up; or by dividends returns. If the price of the ETF position rises, the investor's earning goes high. Alternatively, if the ETF position price goes down, the investor loses money.

If for example you bought an ETF of $40 and after one year the price of the ETF position went up to $50, then you would earn $10 if you sold the ETF. Before investing, it is important to undertake research and oversee which ETFs are performing. Also, consulting with a broker to find out about fees and commission is paramount. Every investment involves a risk and ETFs are no different.

Exercise:

Have you invested in any of the stock markets?

-
-
-
-

Section Ten

Children and money

Where family units with children exist, one also finds the concept of saving for the children. The fact of the matter is that children will eventually manage their own money and you will not have control over this once they mature. However, as they grow older, children often behave according to how they see their parents behave.

If your household is run on debt, that concept is instilled into the people surrounding you, including your children. On the other hand, if you manage your money appropriately and value what you do with it, it trickles down to your children as they learn the same concepts. You become a role model and your children emulate your behaviours.

Some people start putting some money aside for their children when their offspring are young. The first step is to open a bank account in your child's name; however, children cannot operate this account therefore the parents are also registered as an account holder.

Once the account is open, allocate some money to deposit to their account. Even though internet banking has made it easier to use banking services, taking your children with you to the bank to deposit cash makes them feel ownership of their money, which is important.

They enjoy the adventure of just going to the bank and having their own money, particularly if they earn it by doing some small chores at home. Even though in reality they cannot do anything with that money, the experience and the adventure is what counts, and they can watch their savings grow.

Before opening such accounts, it does not hurt to shop around and see which banks have children-friendly bank accounts – the kind that do not attract any fees, can make some interest, and are easy to manage. Interest made through money deposited in the bank incurs government tax and your tax file number is required by the bank so that the taxes are not paid at a higher interest rate.

Upon reaching the teenage stage where children can manage their own accounts, as parents you organise transitional period until you are sure that they can handle their money carefully.

Giving your children responsibility by transferring their money to their own accounts when the age is appropriate makes them feel that they are grown up and that their parents can trust them in managing their own money.

Children are all different, but with luck they will adopt the values you have provided them in life. You will have done your part in nurturing and providing education on everyday life skills.

While it is important to provide a starting point in saving money for your children, don't stress yourself providing luxuries for them. They need to learn the value of money and see that working for it is a responsible and positive thing. Teaching the basics set out in this book will set them up for a positive relationship with money and savings.

Exercise:

Do you have an account for your children? If so, ask them to explain what they understand by having their money in the bank.

-
-
-
-

Getting flexible after job loss due to COVID-19

Pandemics do not happen often. But 2020 year was one of those years where few people could have predicted that COVID-19 was going to ruin many of our lives. The world came to a standstill and many people lost their jobs, not knowing what else they could do. Flexibility is necessary in order to keep meeting daily expenditures.

The ability to be flexible and resilient with change, and willingness to take any type of job, is sometimes necessary. It is better to receive a little bit of money rather than none at all. For those working as pilots, air hostesses, or in travel, hospitality and other businesses where there are few alternative avenues, then even taking farm work would go some way to meeting financial needs.

Another strategy for surviving this terrible period is to evaluate the level of consumption in your household and reduce unnecessary expenditure to save money and stretch the savings for a longer time – until other jobs are available.

Negotiation with your boss could be another way of keeping your job, even though that might mean compromising on hours of work. Opportunities like this are worth taking, rather than going home with nothing. If and when COVID-19 is under control, more work might become available and your boss might keep you on the job. This is what happened to Kelly.

> *Kelly had worked at the airport full-time for 15 years with an airline company, undertaking customer service. However, according to her employer things changed due to the virus and there was no more work available for Kelly.*

> *Kelly was rendered jobless and without a degree to back her up for another job, there was only an opportunity to take a different type of job – still in the airport – explaining to customers what was required by the government to keep everyone safe.*

> *This job was only for 16 hours a fortnight, but Kelly took the offer and even though it brought in less than she was used to earning she still got a little bit of money to keep her going. She has also embarked on looking for another job where she could use her transferrable customer care skills.*

Managing money is always a very sensitive area for most people, couples and families. Some are good at handling even the smallest amount of money and can leverage within their needs and wants. Others might have problems managing money and seek help from financial advisers.

Some just ignore their money issues, and have problems – spiralling into debt since they do not know how to handle their finances, and because they fear being seen as failures.

Whichever category you might be in, always remember there is no perfect way of managing money; however, keeping it simple using planning of budgets, building some savings, identifying areas of investments and enjoying what life has to offer is all it takes.

Exercise:

After reading this book, do you think you have some idea on how you can manage your money?

-

-

-

-

Table 1. An example of a person's yearly budget as discussed earlier

Description	Jan	Feb	March	April	May	June
Income						
Salary	3,500	3,500	3,500	3,500	3,500	3,500
Side business	2,000	900	800	1,000	900	800
Interests	200	100	200	200	150	200
Gifts	150	150	150	150	150	150
Dividends	200					150
Total	6,050	4,650	4,650	4,850	4,700	4,800
Expenses						
Rental/Mortgage	1,000	1,000	1,000	1,000	1,000	1,000
Mobile phone	300	300	300	300	300	300
Utilities						
Electricity	250				400	
Water	250				250	
Gas	200				350	
New refrigerator					1,200	
Personal						
Health insurance	200	200	200	200	200	200
Health products	80	80	80	80	80	80
Gifts	50	50		50	50	
Food						
Groceries	250	250	250	250	250	250
Lunches	80	80	80	80	80	80
Transportation						
Car insurance		1,080				
Maintenance/repairs				250		
Public transport	200	200	200	200	200	200
Licences road	800					
Debts						
Credit card payment	200					200
Entertainment						
Eating out	100	100	100	100	100	100
Movie tickets			300			
Sporting events		200			200	
Gymnastics	250	250	250	250	250	250
Beverages	200	200	200	200	200	200
Pets						
Veterinary expenses	500					
Food	200	200	200	200	200	200
Savings						
Long term goals	250	250	250	250	250	250
Emergencies	200	200	200	200	200	200
Short term projects	100	100	100	100	100	100
Superannuation or retirement	300	300	300	300	300	300
Total expenses	5,960	5,040	4,010	4,010	6,160	3,910
Balance	90	-390	640	840	-1,460	890

Description	July	Aug	Sept	Oct	Nov	Dec	Total
Income							
Salary	3 500	3 500	3 500	3 500	3 500	3 500	42 000
Side business	800	300	1 000	500	700	1 000	10 700
Interests	100	200	50	50	100	100	1 650
Gifts	150	150	150	150	150	150	1 800
Dividends						200	550
Total	4,550	4,150	4,700	4,200	4,450	4,950	56,700
Expenses							
Rental/Mortgage	1 000	1 000	1 000	1 000	1 000	1 000	12 000
Mobile phone	300	300	300	300	300	300	3 600
Utilities							
Electricity			300			300	1 250
Water			250			250	1 000
Gas			200			200	950
Purchase of new refrigerator							1 200
Personal							
Health insurance	200	200	200	200	200	200	2 400
Heath products	80	80	80	80	80	80	960
Gifts			50		50	300	600
Food							
Groceries	250	250	250	250	250	250	3 000
Lunches	80	80	80	80	80	80	960
Transportation							
Car insurance							1 080
Maintenance/repairs		200					450
Publ i c transport	200	200	200	200	200	200	2 400
Licences road							800
Debts							
Credit card payment						200	600
Entertainment							
Eating out	100	100	100	100	100	100	1 200
Movie tickets	300				300		900
Sporting events		200			200		800
Gymnastics	250	250	250	250	250	250	3 000
Beverages	200	200	200	200	200	200	2 400
Pets							
Veterinary expenses			500				1 000
Food	200	200	200	200	200	200	2 400
Savings							
Long term goals	250	250	250	250	250	250	3 000
Emergencies	200	200	200	200	200	200	2 400
Short term projects	100	100	100	100	100	100	1 200
Superannuation or retirement	300	300	300	300	300	300	3 600
Total expenses	4,010	4,110	5,010	3,710	4,260	4,960	55,150
Balance	540	40	-310	490	190	-10	1,550

Did you find this book helpful?

I hope I have educated you to some extent on some fundamental concepts relating to managing money.

Money Tracking Form

Date	Expenditure	Cost	Mode of Payment	Subtotal

Incoming record for six months.

Income	Jan	Feb	Mar	Apr	May	Jun	Total
Salaries							
Interest from savings							
Dividends							
Gifts received							
Other Side business							
Total							

References

Australian Securities Exchange (ASX). (2010). How to Buy and Sell Shares.
https://www.asx.com.au/documents/resources/shares_course_05.pdf?shares_course_05_text

Australian Government, Australian Tax Office. (2019) Government Super Contributions.
https://www.ato.gov.au/Individuals/Super/Growing-your-super/Adding-to-your-super/Government-super-contributions/

Australia Government Bonds. (2019) Exchange-traded Bonds offera way for retail investors to access Australian Government Bonds.
https://www.australiangovernmentbonds.gov.au/

Interest Only Home Loans. (2020) Decide whether interest only home loan is right for you.
https://moneysmart.gov.au/home-loans/interest-only-home- loans